THE AWARD
and Other Plays

Warren Manzi

A SAMUEL FRENCH ACTING EDITION

SAMUELFRENCH.COM
SAMUELFRENCH-LONDON.CO.UK

Copyright © 1999 by Warren Manzi
All Rights Reserved

THE AWARD, ONE FOR THE MONEY, THE QUEEN OF THE PARTING SHOT, THE AUDITION, and *MOROCCAN TRAVEL GUIDE* is fully protected under the copyright laws of the United States of America, the British Commonwealth, including Canada, and all other countries of the Copyright Union. All rights, including professional and amateur stage productions, recitation, lecturing, public reading, motion picture, radio broadcasting, television and the rights of translation into foreign languages are strictly reserved.

ISBN 978-0-573-62686-9
www.SamuelFrench.com
www.SamuelFrench-London.co.uk

For Production Enquiries

United States and Canada
Info@SamuelFrench.com
1-866-598-8449

United Kingdom and Europe
Plays@SamuelFrench-London.co.uk
020-7255-4302

Each title is subject to availability from Samuel French, depending upon country of performance. Please be aware that *TTHE AWARD, ONE FOR THE MONEY, THE QUEEN OF THE PARTING SHOT, THE AUDITION,* and *MOROCCAN TRAVEL GUIDE* may not be licensed by Samuel French in your territory. Professional and amateur producers should contact the nearest Samuel French office or licensing partner to verify availability.

CAUTION: Professional and amateur producers are hereby warned that *THE AWARD, ONE FOR THE MONEY, THE QUEEN OF THE PARTING SHOT, THE AUDITION,* and *MOROCCAN TRAVEL GUIDE* is subject to a licensing fee. Publication of this play(s) does not imply availability for performance. Both amateurs and professionals considering a production are strongly advised to apply to Samuel French before starting rehearsals, advertising, or booking a theatre. A licensing fee must be paid whether the title(s) is presented for charity or gain and whether or not admission is charged. Professional/Stock licensing fees are quoted upon application to Samuel French.

No one shall make any changes in this title(s) for the purpose of production. No part of this book may be reproduced, stored in a retrieval system, or transmitted in any form, by any means, now known or yet to be invented, including mechanical, electronic, photocopying, recording, videotaping, or otherwise, without the prior written permission of the publisher. No one shall upload this title(s), or part of this title(s), to any social media websites.

For all enquiries regarding motion picture, television, and other media rights, please contact Samuel French.

MUSIC USE NOTE

Licensees are solely responsible for obtaining formal written permission from copyright owners to use copyrighted music in the performance of this play and are strongly cautioned to do so. If no such permission is obtained by the licensee, then the licensee must use only original music that the licensee owns and controls. Licensees are solely responsible and liable for all music clearances and shall indemnify the copyright owners of the play(s) and their licensing agent, Samuel French, against any costs, expenses, losses and liabilities arising from the use of music by licensees. Please contact the appropriate music licensing authority in your territory for the rights to any incidental music.

IMPORTANT BILLING AND CREDIT REQUIREMENTS

If you have obtained performance rights to this title, please refer to your licensing agreement for important billing and credit requirements.

THE AWARD AND OTHER PLAYS originally opened Off-Broadway in New York City at Theatre Four on Tuesday, April 2, 1991. It was presented by the Actors Collective: Warren Manzi, Artistic Director; Catherine Russell, Managing Director. The settings and graphics were by Jay Cail Stone, the lighting by Patrick Eagleton, the costumes by Nancy Bush, the sound by David Lawson. the stage manager was Carol Venezia. It was directed by the author, and the program and cast was as follows:

ONE FOR THE MONEY
MAN..Brian Dowd

THE QUEEN OF THE PARTING SHOT
WOMAN...Catherine Russell
HOUSE MANAGER....................................Dean Gardner

intermission

THE AUDITION*
JACK...James Farrell

THE AWARD
MAN...Marcus Powell

*THE AUDITION was re-written and subsequently re-staged, while the production was running, with the following cast:
WOMAN'S VOICE................................Margaret Russell
JACK SINGLETON.......................................David Valcin

PROGRAM AND CHARACTERS

ONE FOR THE MONEY
MAN

*MOROCCAN TRAVEL GUIDE
TOUR GUIDE (man) (voice over)
SLIDE-SHOW HOST (man) (voice over)
FEMALE STAND-UP

THE QUEEN OF THE PARTING SHOT
WOMAN
HOUSE MANAGER

Intermission

THE AUDITION
WOMAN (voice over)
JACK SINGLETON

THE AWARD
MAN

SCENE
There is a table, chair and a phone for the first half that will be exchanged for another table, chair and phone for the second half.
There is a slide screen that appears for the second play.

*MOROCCAN TRAVEL GUIDE was not performed in the original New York production.

"If thou didst ever hold me in thy heart
Absent thee from felicity awhile,
And in this harsh world draw thy breath in pain,
To tell my story."

-*Hamlet*, Act V, Scene II

The Award and Other Plays is dedicated with great love and admiration to my friend, Jay Cail Stone.

October 20, 1998
W.M.

ONE FOR THE MONEY

In the Lobby at the entrances to the theatre are signs that say "Tonight, a representative of the Actors Fund of North America will speak to you". Right after the two-minute warning, a man's voice is heard over the loudspeakers.

MAN'S VOICE
(*on tape*)
    Ladies and Gentlemen, welcome to the theatre. As you take your seats, or while you are reading your programs, you might notice our ushers passing among you. They will be collecting for the Actors Fund of North America. Each year the Actors Fund of North America collects from hundreds of theaters. The custom follows that before the play begins, ushers pass among you; we ask merely what would be acceptable. Thousands of actors depends on us for information, for instruction and for sanctuary. Condominiums in many cities house thousands of low-income or out-of-work actors. Plays are written for them, but most plays do not always fare well in such a competitive market. The Actors Fund of North America...
(*a man is heading down the aisle to the front*)
    ...is proud to serve thousands of actors. Please give generously. Thank you.
(*the man has neared the front, he's wearing a jacket and tie, he's reaching into his jacket pocket*)

MAN
    Ladies and Gentlemen, good evening. Uh, they weren't suppose to play that tonight.
(*pause*)
    They told me the stage manager's sick; someone else did that.
(*he puts on a mask. it's a cat mask with the lower half gone*)

MAN (continued)

I bring you greetings from *CATS*. MEOW MEOW. I apologize for the foul up. They weren't, uh, supposed to play that tonight. Tonight the Actors Fund of North America brings personal greetings. Hold onto your money for a moment, okay?
(pause)

I just came from *CATS*, a sold-out matinee.[1] A truly great musical. The audience loved it. I think there were five curtain calls, people screaming, really living it up.
(pause)

Tonight, we've asked the management to give us thirteen minutes of your time. I realize you might see this as an imposition. You naturally want the play to start. But researchers have found that UNLIKE movie theaters, LIVE theatre collections LIKE THIS actually create a prologue for the audience, as though what I'm saying now were part of the play! So, just consider me a character, okay? The people at *CATS* caught right on—they even asked me to sing a song! HA HA HA! Seriously, the Actors Fund can only exist through your support and your support only: Your support saves lives! And isn't that what it's all about?
(pause)

It reminds me of that story about the watermelon and the Kansas family; but I don't want to detour us from the Actors Fund of North America. After all, it's only through the grace of several endowments that we are even here tonight. I am often asked, "Who shot JFK?" I don't know. And before we collect, let me say that ANYTHING is welcome. Except pennies. It's not funny when you give pennies.

It shows a lack of respect. I'm going to, uh, keep this mask on, uh, I want to use it to explain something later that pertains to

---

[1] **If this is a matinee, or a production outside of NYC, "I saw CATS yesterday; completely sold out."**

MAN (continued)

musicals, and why people like musicals better than plays. The reason I'm asked about JFK, though, is because I played him once. You see, I'm also an actor. And I depend on the Actors Fund for my very existence. When I was preparing to come here tonight my wife said "hey, honey, before you do your demonstration, why don't you read that snappy letter you got from Ontario, as it might be a good lead-in to your presentation." Y'know, she's always right.
(going into his pocket)
 The letter my wife spoke of is from Ontario.
(he produces a letter, he is opening it.)
 I'll just read the whole letter to you, then do that demonstration.
(looking at letter.)
 It's from Ontario, Canada. It gotta crest thing on top of the letter, it's like a dragon, with wings, or a cape, it says ONTARIO PLAYERS; oh the letter is TYPED, it's got DUST all over it. It says "DEAR ACTORS FUND OF NORTH AMERICA, I'm trapped inside this theater. I'm sitting here typing a letter to you. I'm backstage in somebody's office. I was watching *WAITING FOR GODOT*, I fell asleep. I can't get out of this building. It's three a.m. I've got a bottle of Jack Daniels. I read your pamphlet. Will you please tell me WHAT THE HELL IS THE ACTORS FUND OF NORTH AMERICA?"
(looking up)
 My wife loves this letter because of the SYMBOLISM. *WAITING FOR GODOT* is her favorite play. She loves it. Remember in the play, the two guys keep waiting for Godot, but he never shows up? My wife goes nuts over that part. She says it's EXACTLY like life. Life is this one ENORMOUS PLAY: a guy just STARTS TALKING. He's TALKING ABOUT HIGHWAYS. HE'S TALKING ABOUT ADDING WORDS TOGETHER TO FORM SCISSORS, THINK OF MY WIFE, she stops me at the door, she says "read that snappy letter before your fifteen-minute demonstration."

MAN (continued)

I look at her, it's the Godot thing. If we're having muffins and I ask her for the jam, she'll say "If I give you the jam, will you use it BECAUSE I gave it to you?" Let me take this mask off.
(he will.)

I loved *Cats*.
(he puts the mask in his pocket)(pause)

The thing about my wife and the jam comment is the Ontario letter, the letter I just read you. My wife IMAGINES the guy typing in the theater like Godot not showing up, so the JAM COMMENT, the comment about giving me the jam is the same as her wanting me to read the ONTARIO LETTER. It's not that she's making any sense but she can SEIZE THE MOMENT. She really can. I've never been able to do that. WHADDAYA DO? TAKE YOUR MONEY OUT OF YOUR POCKET AND GIVE IT TO ME RIGHT THIS SECOND!"
(pause)

See. Doesn't work for me. I wish those aliens had brought ME to their ship instead of my wife.
(pause)

The people at *CATS* went nuts over that aliens remark. So, to introduce the demonstration I will first outline the entire history of theatre, with a focus on every labor union AND the history of labor. The reason for this is unclear; Uh,
(going into his pocket, putting away the letter and taking out index cards)

actually I do know the reason.
(reading)

"Since most of you come from communities that have amateur theatres, we want to coordinate your labor unions or affiliations with the Actors Fund of North America."
(looking up)

I'm really NOT going to outline the history of theatre, or

MAN (continued)
labor. I said that deliberately to make you uncomfortable.
(pause)

The Actors Fund has created ingenious presentations for evoking audience response. See, actors are the front lines for product—they're foot soldiers carrying various FLAGS from MacDonalds, Paine Weber, from EXXON. Now with our new systems, actors are finally equipped to CONVINCE YOU OF ANYTHING. YOU MUST GIVE GENEROUSLY!
(pause)

Sorry. But if you could visit the Plant with me, you'd know why I got emotional. Ladies and Gentlemen, I really believe in this. I'm not just some SPOKESPERSON. I'm visiting hundreds of theaters this year. It's funny.
(very slight pause)

I told this group at *Death of a Salesman* last week I was going to outline the history of labor, and two guys got up and walked right out, they just got up an' left! THAT'S how good our marketing department is!!
(pause)

Look, my ability to persuade you to contribute five dollars, say, must be equal to KING LEAR'S ability to RAGE about DAUGHTERS or whatever his problem actually is. TAKE YOUR MONEY OUT OF YOUR POCKET AND GIVE IT TO ME!
(pause) (grinning)

That was better, wasn't it?
(slight pause—looking right at someone in the back)

WELL, IT WAS BETTER!
(now to everyone)

One of my bosses is here tonight. They've been ribbing me all week about seizing the moment. Because of that Ontario letter: the letter I just read you. Also because I drive a CIVIC, Honda. They've been telling all of us to buy American. BUY AMERICAN! God, how many times must they tell us? Oh, Thank God, he's finally

MAN (continued)

gone. Ladies and Gentlemen, my boss isn't really here. I've been trying to drive that usher out of this room for the last ten minutes. Oh, and I didn't mean to embarrass you, sir.
(indicating someone in the balcony)
　　Let's have a nice hand for this gentleman who played my boss.
(applauds)
　　I thought that usher would never leave.
(pause)
　　Why are you people here anyway? Look, I loved *Cats*, but that aside, the theatre is a dead issue, isn't it? It's a DINOSAUR. yes, it's a night out, BRING THE KIDS. SHAKESPEARE has his place, but WE HAVE TO GO FORWARD, DON'T WE?
(looking around)
　　Look at this room. look at this stage.
(looking up the aisle)
　　Here comes the usher.
(louder)
　　SO I'M THINKING OF SELLING MY HONDA, AND MY SONY TELEVISION SET—CHRIST, IN TWO YEARS PEOPLE 'LL BE BREAKING MY WINDOWS!
(looking up the aisle)
　　He's gone. I'm not trying to undermine, here, but ACTORS are suffering. LOOK, when you do television or MOVIES, YOU'RE PLAYING TO THE CAMERA, IT'S GLASS. YOU'RE PLAYING TO YOURSELF, YOU CAN REHEARSE IT AT HOME. ALSO, IF MISTAKES ARE MADE, THERE'S CONTROL. ON TV THEY EDIT, THEY ADD MUSIC, THEY SPLIT-SCREEN. SAME WITH MOVIES; how much did you pay for your tickets tonight? FOR WHAT? Not too many SPECIAL EFFECTS TONIGHT, HUH?
(looking up the aisle)

MAN (continued)

Here he comes again. The Japanese are CRUSHING US COMMERCIALLY—WE HAVE TO FIGHT BACK—WE HAVE TO SELL BETTER! YOU DON'T KNOW WHAT YOU LIKE! WHY DO YOU THINK THE MOST EXPENSIVE STUFF IN THE SUPERMARKET IS ALWAYS ON THE EASIEST SHELF TO REACH? BECAUSE IT'S THE EASIEST SHELF TO REACH! AND YOU THOUGHT *WAITING FOR GODOT* WAS COMPLICATED?
(looking)
   He just left again.
(pause)
   When I'm in a bigger theater, I speak SUBLIMINALLY, because the ushers usually hang around; I'm dead serious about this theatre business though.
(pause)
   Actors don't make money working in the theatre; it's a self-defeating process; there's no OUTCOME; NOTHING IS ACCOMPLISHED — On television, the sponsorship is VISIBLE, good, we have, maybe HALLMARK PRESENTS *WAITING FOR GODOT* —good—GODOT DOESN'T SHOW UP, FINE, we still have HALLMARK GREETING CARDS—GOOD—SO I GO OUT AND BUY HALLMARK—THE MONEY GOES TO HALLMARK, HALLMARK PAYS THE ACTORS—VERY GOOD! NOW THE ACTOR HAS PURPOSE—SELL HALLMARK—WAIT FOR GODOT ALL YOU WANT, BUT SELL HALLMARK!!
(pause)
   Movies involve multi-corporate sponsorship, but I don't have to go into all that; you understood my example. The Actors Fund of North America is training actors at this very moment—we need them on the front lines, we don't want them DICKING AROUND IN THEATERS LIKE THIS! I'm sorry I get so depressed in rooms like this, it's almost laughable.

MAN (continued)
(looking up the aisle) (quieter)
Here he comes again.
(louder)
Ladies, YOU HAVE AN ASSEMBLY-LINE MENTALITY—when you buy a dress you think you're choosing the dress you want? All you're doing is SELECTING ONE; Your home doesn't REFLECT your individuality, you live in a MESS OF OTHER PEOPLE'S CHOICES. Does this make you HAPPY?
(looking up the aisle)
He's gone.
(pause)
No, he's not.
(slight pause)
He was never there.
(pause)
This is called our SPLIT-SCREEN presentation.
(slight pause)
Audience manipulation traces it's roots directly to Coca Cola;
(reading from his index cards)
"Use a hand gesture when you read this"—UH, No, I wasn't supposed to say that, OBVIOUSLY, HA HA HA HA HA HA,
(looking down, reading)
"Audience manipulation is the easiest way..."
(looks up quickly) See, this PROVES what I was saying about this ROOM—If I were on FILM YOU WOULDN'T HAVE KNOWN I MADE THAT MISTAKE. That was pretty stupid when I goofed that line. "USE A HAND GESTURE WHEN YOU READ THIS"—HA HA HA
(pause)
Let me put these away.
(putting index cards away, they hit his jacket and fall to the floor.)
OH GOD!
(he bends down to pick them up.)

MAN (continued)
I'M SO SORRY, LADIES AND GENTLEMEN, THIS IS REALLY..., I'VE NEVER...,
(he's picking up index cards)
I've blown the whole thing, HAVEN'T I?
(he stands, puts cards away) (pause)
I have three children.
(pause)
Put your money away now. They don't even WANT your money.
(pause)
I was supposed to recite this big speech about Audience manipulation and then STORM OUT—So you wouldn't think it was part of the demonstration.
(slight pause)
Obviously I can't do that now. I've lost the momentum.
(slight pause)
So, I'll just tell you, uh, WHY I was going to STORM out—then you can go on with the show. I'll leave, I mean.
(pause)
THAT'S what's been bothering me. They asked me to turn the house lights down when I leave. How can I storm out if I have to turn down the house lights when I go?
(slight pause)
It's because the stage manager's sick. She's sick.
LOOK, I DON'T CARE ABOUT THE ACTORS FUND, I HAVE THREE CHILDREN AND A WIFE, IT'S A FANTASTIC JOB, I'M ASKING YOU TO GO ALONG WITH ME. I SCREWED UP, I ADMIT IT, SO LET'S QUIT EVEN. WHY ARE YOU LOOKING AT ME LIKE THAT? YOU THINK THIS IS PART OF THE ACT? IF YOU TELL THEM I SCREWED UP, I'M GONNA GET FIRED! I didn't write that other stuff, don't be mad at ME.
(slight pause)

MAN (continued)

This isn't even my suit I'm wearing. I'll tell you this much, I couldn't afford to see this play. I couldn't afford to see *CATS*. Let alone take my family.

(slight pause)

I'd have to get half-price tickets. Even then, I couldn't take all my kids. I'd have to get a baby sitter. You people are NUTS for coming here tonight.

(pause)

You think I'm still doing my BIT. SEE, YOU'VE FALLEN INTO THEIR TRAP. You and I are in a MARKETING REVOLUTION AND YOU'RE LOSING BECAUSE YOU DON'T EVEN KNOW IT'S GOING ON! WHY IS THE THEATRE A DINOSAUR? BECAUSE IT'S NOT MARKETABLE, IT CAN'T BE MASS PRODUCED, NO CLOSE-UPS FOR PRODUCTS, AND WHAT'S REALLY DANGEROUS TO THEM IS THEY DON'T WANT YOUR VALUES INTERFERED WITH—THEY'LL TELL YOU WHAT YOU LIKED AND WHY YOU LIKED IT!

(slight pause)

Still, there's so few of you theatre-goers left, they're not really THAT worried. If they were worried, they would've sent one of the TOP guys to talk to you. But they didn't.

(pause)

I've been having a lot of money problems lately, uh, that's why I made that mistake, when I dropped the, uh, index cards on the floor. I could be fired for that. They wouldn't blink twice about firing me.

(slight pause)

It's humiliating when you can't JUST QUIT, isn't it?

(slight pause)

Here we are, in a FREE society, finally,

(pulling cash out of his pocket)

and we let THIS put a STRANGLEHOLD ON OUR INTEGRITY. WHEN MY KIDS OR MY WIFE LOOK ME IN THE

ONE FOR THE MONEY

MAN (continued)
EYE, THEY DON'T SEE CONFIDENCE—TWO OF MY KIDS GO TO SCHOOL WITH ONE OF MY BOSSES KIDS—I'M AFRAID OF WHAT I SAY IN MY OWN HOUSE—
(holding up cash, waiving it)
    THIS IS ALL I THINK ABOUT WHEN I GO TO SLEEP. I WANT MY IMAGINATION BACK! I WANT MY WIFE TO ADMIRE ME AGAIN! HERE!
(he throws the cash into the air over the audience, it falls)
(pause)
    I CAN'T BELIEVE I DROPPED those index cards. Oh, feel free to take the money, they were mainly ones, it's not much, but you can keep it.
(slight pause)
    My wife WAS taken by aliens.
(slight pause)
    SHE believes it.
(slight pause)
    She was gone for almost a whole night. When I woke up in bed, she was next to me. She wasn't the same, though.
(pause)
    I know I could reach her. If I could just, uh, QUIT my job. But if I QUIT, then it's REALLY about money. It's just TOO LATE! I'd have to start again!
(looks at his watch)
    Oops. Look at the time. Well, thank you, Ladies and Gentlemen. Time for me to say farewell.
(slight pause)(looking around)
    Could I just have three or four dollars back? I need to catch a bus. And I'm out of cigarettes.
(slight pause)
    Thanks. Uh, I hope there'll be NO COMPLAINTS about my presentation.
(he starts walking up the aisle)

MAN (continued)
LISTEN TO MY VOICE AS I WALK AWAY. Sorry. That's a marketing trick.
(he's in the back of the theatre)
They asked me to turn the house lights down when I finished.
(there is a brownout)
OWWW! Shit! Oh, I'm terribly sorry Ladies and Gentlemen. My girlfriend always says, "If you drag your feet, you're gonna get a shock.", an' I never listen!

Lemme just turn these lights down. Well, enjoy the show! Thanks again!
(pause)(the house lights and the preset slowly go out)
I burnt my stupid finger!
(he goes out)(pause)
(he comes back in)
I meant my wife!
(he goes out again, laughing)
(pause)

(The play is over.)

MOROCCAN TRAVEL GUIDE

(In the darkness a man's laugh can be heard fading away, a boat on water, oar locks, a cave, a boat moving slowly on water, calming.)

TOUR GUIDE (voice over)

A man is heard laughing in the distance. Our boat has just entered the cave. A slight wind blows around our shoulders. The cave itself possesses singular aspects worth noting.
(The sounds of birds in the distance.)

In winter, the cormorants visit, settling their temporary nests for the coming spring. Their nocturnal arrival confirms that the dormant foliage will soon nurture most of the bird-life in the vicinity. Even large cranes partake of this late winter feast, sometimes losing their way in the extreme darkness.
(the sounds of the oar locks continue, the boat is moving, birds in the distance)

Muskrats often drown trying to reach the foliage, their young, becoming confused, often die of exposure during the long winter.
(more bird sounds, the boat moves on)

Parakeets seem to flock to the south-western corner of the cave—to this day, it is still a mystery as to why.
(slight pause)

As we proceed, you should sense the presence of gigantic stalactites above you, representing millions of years of cave-like development. Back in the theater, a slide show is beginning.
(The cave sounds stop completely. The quiet humming of a slide projector is heard. Suddenly, a slide appears on a screen. A slide-show host will address us. He is somewhere on the stage, unseen.)

SLIDE-SHOW HOST (voice over)

May we have the first slide, please?
(A slide appears on the screen. Bright day. Long shot. Two women walking out of a grocery store, they are both carrying bags. It's a summer's day. Both women are wearing white shorts, tank tops, both women are in their thirties, they appear to be speaking to each

other. Both women wear sunglasses.)
SLIDE-SHOW HOST (voice over)
The woman on the right's name is:
A. Betty
B. Letitia
C. Joan
Next slide, please.

(The same sequence, a few seconds later. The two women are approaching a parking lot. The store is still visible behind them. The two women are still walking together.)
SLIDE-SHOW HOST (voice over) (continuing)
The woman on the left is:
A. Planning a dinner party
B. Joan's best friend
C. A stranger Joan met in the store

(slight pause)

Next slide, please.

(Another slide appears. The same sequence, a few seconds later. The two women are approaching a row of three cars.)
SLIDE-SHOW HOST (voice over) (continuing)
A. Approaching the same car
B. About to have an argument
C. Unaware of the man who is following them

(The screen fades to black. Birds are heard. The sound of a boat on water. Oar locks. We're back in the cave.)
TOUR GUIDE (voice over)
In spring, the cormorants migrate west, raising their young in the pleasing climate of the rocky cliffs. many legends surround the existence of this cave, dating back to the fifth century A.D. One of the more famous legends occurred in 1758, with a certain pirate ship called the *Blue Buccaneer*. It is known as the Legend of Sneaky Kate.

(Gulls are heard calling in the distance. The boat moves on. Oar

locks on water. Movement.)
TOUR GUIDE (voice over)(continued)
Sneaky Kate disguised herself as a man, and stowed away on the *Blue Buccaneer*, as it set sail. That infamous pirate ship feared all over the Atlantic — attacking and pillaging unsuspecting crafts — This particular encounter involved the Spanish Royal Cruiser, *Orontes*, filled with gold bullion, doubloons, trinkets and rich finery. That battle took place on the night of May 17, 1758, two miles from this cave. Back in the theater, the slide show continues.
(The cave sounds suddenly stop. A slide appears on the screen.)(The same sequence. A few seconds later. The woman who is not Joan is about to open the trunk of her car. Joan is standing next to her. Far behind them, a man wearing a Yankees cap is exiting the store. He also wears sunglasses. He is heading in their direction.)
SLIDE-SHOW HOST (voice over)
The man leaving the store is:

A. Joan's husband

B. A serial killer

C. An off-duty police detective

Next slide, please.

(slight pause)

(Another slide appears. The same sequence. A few seconds later. The man seems to be heading toward the two women. The woman who opened the trunk has turned toward Joan. Joan has leaned into her, as though sharing a secret.)
SLIDE-SHOW HOST (voice over)
As Joan's husband approaches, Arlene's sister is whispering to Joan about:

A. the sexual encounter they had yesterday afternoon

B. The fact that Joan's husband is fooling around with Arlene

C. Arlene's attempted suicide

Next slide, please.

(Another slide appears. The same sequence. A few seconds later. Joan's husband is approaching the car. The two women have turned

to look at him. He appears to be smiling.)
SLIDE-SHOW HOST
The three people in this photograph are unaware that:
A. A bomb is about to go off
B. The store is about to be robbed
C. A thunderstorm is about to occur

(The screen fades to black. The sounds of a boat on water, oar locks, birds crying, calm.)
TOUR GUIDE (voice over)
In disguise, as a gunner's mate, Kate took part in that fateful battle. Cannon blazing. Loading and reloading until the *Orontes* surrendered in a cloud of smoke. the pirates buried most of the treasure nearby. But one chest of gold was unaccounted for. They all assumed it had sank to the bottom, but it hadn't. Somehow, Kate had snuck it away. Back in the theater a female stand-up is about to perform.

(The cave sounds suddenly stop. A spotlight goes on, pointing at the left side of the stage. A young woman stands there. She is in her early twenties, her hair is black, purple and yellow. She wears purple leather, she holds a long black cordless microphone, with a metal antenna sticking out of the bottom of it.)
FEMALE STAND-UP
YEAH, SO I'M ON THE OPERATING TABLE, RIGHT, CHECK THIS OUT, THIS BIG FUCKING NURSE IS TICKLING MY FEET—NOT LIKE KOOCHI-KOO BUT FUCKING TICKLING MY FEET—SO I WAKE UP, RIGHT, I'M FIEND'N MAN—MY ALARM'S GOIN' NUTS, DAYLIGHTS KILLIN' ME, I'M STARING, CHECK THIS OUT, I'M STARING AT MY REFRIGERATOR, THIS FUCKING NOTE I LEFT MYSELF—BIG LETTERS, REAL EMPHATIC—"KENNEDY—ELEVEN A.M.", MAN I HAVE NO FUCKING IDEA—"KENNEDY—ELEVEN A.M." RIGHT, RIGHT—AIRPORT—GOTTA DO IT—SO WHAT'S THE DEAL—MY GUY, MY DRIVER—HE'S HISTORY—CAN'T CALL HIM—LIKE OH NO—GOTTA CAB

FEMALE STAND-UP (continued)

IT—SHIT—GOTTA GET TO THE AIRPORT—SHIT—CHECK THIS OUT—**NO HOT WATER IN THE SHOWER—FUCK ME**—I'M JONES'N—NO TIME—BUT I LOOK GREAT—LIKE SHIT—BUT GREAT—FUCK—IT'S FRIDAY, WHAT'S UP WITH THIS—THE FUCKING VICE PRESIDENT'S IN TOWN—FUCK—NEW YORK? YOU NEVER BEEN THERE? CHILL—IT'S FUCK'N MADNESS—MY GIG'S IN MOROCCO TOMORROW, GOTTA FLY—SO I'M ON FORTY THIRD HAILING CABS—THIS BIG FUCKING DUDE STOPS—CHECK THIS OUT—IS HE HAIRY? FUCK ME— I JUMP IN—TRAFFIC IS BULLSHIT—WHAT'S UP WITH THIS? THE FUCKING VICE PRESIDENT'S HERE—I SHOULD SLIT MY WRISTS, RIGHT—SO I'M IN THE CAB—WE'RE FUCKING DEAD STOPPED—MIDDLE OF SUMMER—NO AIR CONDITIONING—DEAD STOPPED— GUY RECOGNIZES ME—"HEY, I KNOW YOU!" SHIT LIKE THAT—LIKE HE CHECKED OUT MY NEW VIDEO—Y'KNOW—"DADDY DEAREST" — FUCK—HE LOVES MY SHIT—GET THIS CAB MOVIN—DUDE—I'M JONES'N—I TELL'M—GOT TO GET TO MOROCCO—SEE, HE THINKS I'M JUST A SINGER—Y'KNOW "DADDY DEAREST" "STEAL MY HEART" "WHO'S YOUR BEST BITCH?"—THAT'S HOW HE SEES ME—AND THE FUCKIN' VICE PRESIDENT'S IN TOWN AND WE ARE CRAWLING UP THE FDR—THIS BIG FUCKING HAIRY DUDE IS HUMMING MY SHIT LIKE I'M SUPPOSED TO APPLAUD HIM—WHAT'S UP WITH THIS—SO I TELL HIM I'M A PERFORMANCE ARTIST—SHIT—WHAT? A MARTIAN? A VENUTIAN?—I'M GOIN' TO MOROCCO—THAT'S THE GIG—HE'S STILL SINGING MY SHIT—THEN HE STOPS, LIKE, OH NO—SOCIAL COMMENTARY?! FUCK ME— I GOT NO TIMEPIECE ON ME AND HIS FUCKIN DASHBOARD DIGITAL IS SO SMALL, I'D HAVE TO BE BLOWING HIM TO SEE IT—FUCK—SO HE GETS MY POINT ABOUT

FEMALE STAND-UP (continued)
THE SOCIAL SHIT—MAN, HE SNAPS—BIG FUCKING HAIRY DUDE STARTS EXPOUNDING—WE'RE BOTH SWEAT'N LIKE PIGS—FUCKING VICE PRESIDENT—IF YOU'VE NEVER LIVED IN NEW YORK YOU HAVE NO IDEA WHAT TRAFFIC IS LIKE—IMAGINE THOUSANDS OF TINY INSECTS ON YOUR COFFEE TABLE—THOUSANDS OF THEM ALL BUNCHED UP MOVING SLOWLY, THOUSANDS OF INSECTS ON YOUR COFFEE TABLE—AND IT'S HOT—IT'S THE HOTTEST FUCKING DAY EVER AND I'M FIEND'N AND THIS ASSHOLE IS SINGING "WHO'S YOUR BEST BITCH?"—OFF KEY—THEN HE GETS IT—HE' PISSED ABOUT THE TRAFFIC, THE VICE PRESIDENT'S IN TOWN—WHAT'S UP WITH THIS? WE'RE JUST ABOUT ON THE BRIDGE—HE STARTS ASKIN ME ABOUT MOONS—WELL, YAH; WHAT? FUCKIN HAIRY DUDE, MAN, TALKING ABOUT MOONS? WHAT'S UP WITH THIS? YOU MEAN LIKE ANY MOON? NO—MAN—THIS GUY'S, LIKE INFORMED—AND BULLSHIT—LIKE IT'S A FUCKING CAUSE! HE'S SAYIN' SHIT LIKE —CHECK THIS OUT—JUPITER—WELL, YAH, BIG FUCKING PLANET, RIGHT? LIKE JUPITER'S MOONS—HELLO!? THEY'RE SATELLITES HE SAYS—YAH? CHECK THIS OUT—LIKE GANNYMEADE, CALLISTO—FUCK—WHAT? ELARA—SHIT—BLOW ME—THIS FUCKIN' DUDE IS JONES'N, MAN—THEN HE'S TALKIN' ABOUT SATURN—YEAH, NICE RINGS—BUT MORE MOONS, MAN, PHOEBE, CALYPSO—SHIT—WE CLEARED THE BRIDGE—STRAIGHT HIGHWAY TO KENNEDY AND THIS MOTHERFUCKER'S DOIN' A LITANY ON ME—TRAFFIC IS STILL BULLSHIT—URANUS? GROTTY, MAN, GROTTÉ, LIKE FIVE MOONS—CHECK THIS OUT—SHAKESPEARE LAND, MIRANDA, ARIEL, OBERON—LIKE WHAT? MARS HAS PHOBOS AND DEIMOS—NOW WE'RE STILL HEAVILY INTO TRAFFIC HERE—IF I MISS THE FLIGHT I LOSE THE GIG—

FEMALE STAND-UP (continued)
GOTTA GET TO MOROCCO AND THIS MOTHERFUCKER STOPS THE CAR TO ILLUSTRATE HIS POINT—SO WHAT'S UP WITH THIS? HE'S TALKIN' SOME SELF DEPRECATING SHIT ABOUT THE PLANET ABOUT US—WELL, YAH—WHO WOKE YOU THE FUCK UP? BUT HE'S GOT A GOOD POINT—WE'VE GOT NO FUCKIN' NAME FOR OUR MOON —IT'S MOON—SHIT IT'S MOON—IT'S NOT HAMLET—BULLWINKLE—IT'S MOON—THAT'S SO FUCKING DEPRESSING—ESPECIALLY STUCK IN TRAFFIC ON THE HOTTEST DAY EVER WITH THE VICE PRESIDENT CRUISING ALONG IN HIS AIR CONDITIONED HUGE FUCKING LIMO HAVING PHONE SEX WITH SOME BIMBO WHO RIDICULES HIS TWO-INCH LIMP DICK BEHIND HIS BACK—WE INSECTS ACKNOWLEDGE OUR INSIGNIFICANCE BY DUBBING OUT PLANET'S BEAUTIFUL SATELLITE WITH THE MOST GENERIC NAME IN THE UNIVERSE—"MOON"—FUCK, MAN, WE'RE ALMOST TO THE AIRPORT—
(she looks at her watch)
SHIT I GOTTA MAKE A CALL—BE RIGHT BACK—
(She goes offstage quickly. The spotlight goes out. The room is black. The sound of a boat on water, oar locks, birds crying.)
TOUR GUIDE (voice over)
In summer, the cormorants return with the parakeets. As a footnote to that famous battle: years later, Kate wrote to her brother in England—it seems she smuggled a small chest of gold off the *Orontes* and buried it in this cave. She died of pneumonia before she could recover it. to this day, researchers and divers still comb the area for SNEAKY KATE'S GOLD—Back in the theater, the slide show continues—
(Another slide appears. The same sequence. A few minutes later. Arlene's sister, Joan, and Joan's husband are sitting in the car—it's raining, a thunderstorm. Joan and Arlene's sister are sitting in the

front seat. Joan's husband is in the back. the car is facing us as it pulls away from the store. Windshield wipers in motion.)
SLIDE-SHOW HOST (voice over)
Arlene's sister is going to:
A. Drop Joan and her husband off at home
B. Invite Joan and her husband over
C. Tell Joan's husband she's been having an affair with Joan
Next slide, please.

(Another slide appears. The same sequence. A few moments later. Thunderstorm rain. The car is gone. Standing under an awning in front of the store is a seven year old girl.)
SLIDE-SHOW HOST (voice over) (continuing)
The little girl is:
A. Waiting for her parents
B. Looking for her nanny
C. Lost

(The screen goes black. The female stand-up is walking quickly out of the wings. A spotlight goes on, on her.)
FEMALE STAND-UP
(entering, quickly looking at watch)
FUCK'N AGENTS, MAN. I INTERRUPT MY GIG, I CALL THEM ON TIME—FUCK'N HOLD ON; MAN—YEAH, SURE—CHECK THIS OUT—THEY PUT ROLLO ON; WHO THE FUCK'S ROLLO? WHERE'S **MY** GUY? "WELL, YAH, HI, NICE TO MEET YOU." FUCK'N ROLLO—I DON'T HAVE TIME FOR THIS SHIT—MY CAREER IS TAKING OFF—I GOTTA JUMP-START MY RESUMÉ SO THIS DICKWAD CAN CATCH UP ON HOMEWORK HE SHOULD'VE DONE TEN MONTHS AGO? FUCK ME!
(slight pause)
YEAH, SO WE GET TO KENNEDY AIRPORT, RIGHT—REAL BUSY—**TRY'N FIND THE FUCKING TERMINAL**—MOROCCAN AIR LINES—WELL YAH! THEY'RE NOT **IN** ALPAHBETICAL ORDER—SURE,   UNITED, TWA—IT'S

FEMALE STAND-UP (continued)
BLOW ME ORDER—EAST COMMUTER AIRWAYS—ACME BULLSHIT AIRLINES—OH, HERE WE GO—STOP THE CAR ASSHOLE—HE'S STILL TALKING ABOUT MOONS! SO I'M TRYIN' TO BUST THROUGH THE DOORS, AN' THE COPS'VE GOT THIS GUY HANDCUFFED, THEY'RE MOVIN' HIM TOWARDS THE EXIT—HE'S DRUNK OUT OF HIS MIND—SCREAMING AT EVERYBODY—AND THERE'S A CHICK BEHIND HIM WITH A BLACK EYE AND A FAT LIP; SHE'S FOLLOWING HIM AND THE COPS—SHE'S DRUNK TOO—SCREAMING—"I LOVE HIM!—HE DIDN'T MEAN IT!YOU FUCKING PIG BASTARDS CAN SUCK MY PUSSY ALL FUCKING NIGHT!" Now, I'm just about late for my flight—this chick starts screaming at me "HELP HIM! HELP HIM!" So, I make my flight. I'm in first class. The only major drawback is sitting next to me for seven fucking hours—THIS BIG FAT FUCK—LOOKS AND SMELLS LIKE THAT FAT FUCKING NURSE IN MY NIGHTMARE.
(slight pause)
Other than that it was a very pleasant flight. We didn't crash or nothin'.
(looking at her watch)
Listen, I gotta book. Ciao.
(she walks offstage. The spotlight goes out.)
(The cave sounds return. The boat, oar locks, birds, peaceful sounds.)
TOUR GUIDE (voice over)
As autumn approaches, the local greenery has begun to turn wondrously orange and pink. Many colorful leaves adorn the nearby cliff. On behalf of the management, staff and crew; as well as our slide-show host and female performance artist; we thank you for joining our tour today. Back in the theater another play is about to begin.
(Slowly, the sounds fade.)

(The play is over.)

THE QUEEN OF THE PARTING SHOT

(In the darkness. After a pause.)
WOMAN
(on phone)

YOU DON'T KNOW ANYTHING ABOUT *Alice in Wonderland*! SARAH, JUST CLOSE YOUR LIPS A SECOND, WILLYA?
(the lights have started up; an old woman holding a newspaper, on the phone)
(slight pause)

I'm on page THREE half-way down. Take the gum outta your mouth—I bet LEO wrote this. HIS FATHER WOULD SPIN IN HIS CASKET! It says "That brilliant actress Sally Moreau." My paper has GOD DAMN INK SMUDGES! Read it, Sarah.
(suddenly)

IS SOMEONE ELSE ON THIS LINE?
(slight pause)

I DON'T CARE THAT YOU'RE MODERNIZING THE SYSTEM! I'M HAVING A PERSONAL CONVERSATION, MISSY! WHY DON'T I JUST LEAVE MY FRONT DOOR OPEN ALL DAY!
(slight pause)

Is she gone, Sarah?
(slight pause)

Will you lose your job?
(slight pause)

Yes, but you can't get drunk at WORK. Read the article. WHO was Alice? SHE was Alice?
(slight pause)

I'M NOT ASKING YOUR OPINION, SARAH, I'M FLYING BLIND HERE!
(slight pause)

I CARE ABOUT YOUR PROBLEMS! I'M HAVING NIGHTMARES! D'YOU THINK I'M JUST KILLING TIME WITH YOU ON THE PHONE?

(slight pause)
WOMAN (continued)
THEY'D NEVER FIRE YOU! I WATCH TELEVISION! THEY GOTTA SELL *PEOPLE* NOW! WE TRIED DIRECT DIALING, REMEMBER?
(slight pause)
What nightmare? Oh, it's been all week. I rush onto a stage, it's outside, there's kids. I sing a STUPID song, then getta heart-attack! But THE KIDS GO CRAZY, APPLAUDING. NO, IT'S TRUE—I MEAN, I THINK IT REALLY HAPPENED! I KEEP HUMMING THAT SONG,
(singing)
'DA DA DOUGHNUTS FROM CAIRO" NO, YOU'RE HUMMING *WHITE CHRISTMAS*! WAIT A MINUTE! READ THE ARTICLE, SARAH! C'MON!
(slight pause)
Sally Moreau was in Buffalo, RIGHT! But she wasn't a star yet.
(slight pause)
People were chosen to go to Buffalo, Sarah; it was a GOVERNMENT thing.
(slight pause)
ALICE IN WONDERLAND! WE PERFORMED *ALICE IN WONDERLAND*! THAT'S HOW WE MET SALLY MOREAU! BUT SHE WASN'T ALICE!
(pause)
I was Alice.
(slight pause)
SARAH, GET ME DOCTOR FITZJAMES! HURRY!
(slight pause)
And let me do the talking if his wife answers. HELLO, MRS. FITZJAMES! IS SOMEBODY MOWING YOUR LAWN? Hello, Doctor. Get off the line Sarah. Am I bothering you, Doctor? OH NOW THE MOWING IS STARTING AGAIN! Well, you gotta

WOMAN (continued)
expect phone calls. What if I'd collapsed on the rug? No, now you made me forget why I called!
(suddenly)

Alice in Wonderland. Remember 50 years ago when we met Sally Moreau? Didn't I play Alice? Don't start coughing—Weren't you one of the fat brothers? Leo says SHE played Alice! SAY THAT AGAIN! THE BUFFALO RETREAT—
(hangs up)(crying)

He had no right printing that reminder!
(picks up phone)

Sarah, get me Leo—SO IT'S YOU AGAIN—Is Bell Atlantic just marching into people's living rooms? WELL, WHERE'S SARAH? Poor girl works a million hours and you FIRE her—Why? Because she drinks? She loses at poker?—WHY DIDN'T YOU TELL ME SHE WAS ON A COFFEE BREAK? GET ME LEO AT THE NEWSPAPER—HELLO? LEO? I'M SUING YOU FOR LIBEL! Oh your father couldn't remember his own name! He kept a diary? REALLY?
(slight pause)

Say that again. Not Dulcie Winterson. I certainly know Dulcie Winterson. I mean the boy's name. Say it again.
(slight pause)

Again?
(slight pause)(hangs up)(crying)

NOW I REMEMBER THAT WHOLE STUPID WEEK!
(singing)

"Da da da da. DOUGHNUTS FROM CAIRO."
(picks up phone)

Sarah? Who the hell asked you to read me that Sally Moreau article?
(she's crying)

Oh, Sarah, I haven't thought about him in years! I NEVER LOVED ANYONE THE WAY—I don't care that you don't know

WOMAN (continued)
what I'm talking about! Sarah, keep talking.
(standing)
　　Don't panic, Sarah, I'm just standing up. Listen, I told that Bell Atlantic woman you play poker—IT WAS AN ACCIDENT I WAS TALKING TOO FAST—No, no NO NO YOU'RE BREAKING MY TRAIN OF THOUGHT! I was telling you about the Buffalo retreat! Hello? Hi, what happened? You mean you deliberately threw your receiver on the floor? Excuse me, headphones, headphones! WHAT LAST STRAW? You're lucky I'm even conversing with you! GOODBYE!
(hangs up)(pause)
　　Now I remember!
(singing)
　　　"Doughnuts from Cairo; Smooching with Spiro
　　　Underneath the Ottoman moon
　　　The blue dress you spoke of—
　　　A true mess with joke love—
　　　From Cairo
　　　The hi-lo casino was never like this!
　　　So kick them if they move again—Oh—
　　　Dollars or doughnuts—
　　　Who cares?"
　　　AHHH!
(grabs her chest)
(knocks over phone)
　　I'm having a violent heart attack! Ahhh! Ahhh!
(falls down, knocking over chair)
(grabs phone)
　　SARAH? DON'T CALL THE HOSPITAL. AFTER MY BIG FINISH I USED TO GRAB MY CHEST AND FAKE A HEART ATTACK—BIG FINISH—BIG FINISH—GET THE WAX OUT OF YOUR EARS! Is somebody else on the line? Emergency break-in from Leo? C'mon, Missy, you're just sitting there on your

WOMAN (continued)

fat butt, taking notes! What's your name, dear? Bathena? What is that, some generic fruit product? Hello, Leo? Did she hang up? What footnote? Your father's diary has a footnote? And?
(sitting slowly)

Oh, God. I shouldn't't've attempted my big finish. Keep reading, Leo.
(slight pause)

See, Sarah, it was during the Great Depression. We joined a wonderful company of actors in Buffalo. The president devised all these great programs to get us back to work—The FEDERAL THEATRE ACT—Imagine, Sarah, middle-class people like us ACTING IN A PLAY—Dulcie Winterson was spectacular—she played the Duchess—get off the line, Sarah, I'll click you when I need you, hurry. Are you alright, Leo? I've never said your father was a jerk—He was a GOOFBALL, THE MAN HURLED HIMSELF DOWN STONE STEPS TO MAKE PEOPLE LAUGH— WHAT'S THE IQ RANGE HERE? He didn't want to be a reporter, Leo! He was desperately unhappy his entire life! Could you read me the footnote now?
(slight pause)

Go back. HE DOESN'T SAY WHO THE WOMAN IS? REALLY?
(standing)

NO—THAT'S ME, NOT SALLY MOREAU—BECAUSE I remember—I remember the hydrangeas, the McKinley Hotel—We ate breakfast in a huge dining room FILLED with windows—THE CAUCUS RACE—I REMEMBER THE CAUCUS RACE—

The costumes had to get wet! I made parrot wings—HA HA HA! I glued—stop crying, Leo! I glued feathers but when he ran out of the lake he had just these cardboard arms—Hello?
(clicks receiver)(quickly)

LEO?
(quickly)

Sarah? Oh, thank God, Bathena! You must find Dulcie

WOMAN (continued)

Winterson! Don't hang up! What? You mean just now? They just FIRED HER? REALLY?

(slight pause)

Yes, of course she drinks. I wouldn't say compulsive gambler. SARAH WAS NEVER A FRIEND OF MINE—DID SHE TELL YOU THAT? Listen, Bathena, would you get me Dulcie Winterson before I die of old age? HA HA HA HA Yes I hear it ringing. Get off the line now, Bathena. THANK YOU. HANG UP, BATHENA!

(pause)

Hello, Dulcie Winterson? Yes—what a memory you have! Did you see that Rita Miller died? I know it's been ten years, Dulcie—I—I thought you were mad at—we didn't have a fight, Dulcie. A fight is when you knock someone's teeth out—NO—TEN YEARS AGO YOU THREW A MARTINI IN MY FACE, ELEVEN YEARS AGO, I DUMPED THE SPAGHETTI IN YOUR LAP—YES—YES I WANT TO RESOLVE IT TOO—THAT'S WHY I'M CALLING YOU—I DIDN'T LEAD HIM ON! He followed me from Buffalo!—I NEVER TOLD HIM I LOVED HIM! Listen to me, Dulcie, Leo's father kept a diary! STOP TALKING ABOUT THE BOY! YOU'VE NEVER LET A MAN TOUCH YOU, SO I DON'T KNOW WHO MADE YOU THE BOSS OF ROMANCE!

(House Manager enters)

Well, you started it. It was a game to me, Dulcie. Sally Moreau wanted him. Sally Moreau made it a contest. That's why I let him follow me back here! That's why I led him on. When he showed up I told him to beat it or I'd call the cops!

(laughs) (slight pause)(speaking to auditorium)

Is my cab here?

(slight pause)

HOUSE MANAGER

Yes, but it's the Pakistani.

(pause)

WOMAN
(smiling)
Give me a minute.
(back into phone)
What did you say, Dulcie? Goonie? Who the hell're you talking about? Goonie! OH YAH! She was Sally Moreau's dresser! She had a crush on him too, remember? HA HA Goonie was supposed to meet him one night, but I put sleeping tablets in her cocoa and I went instead! Ha ha ha! Goonie! 'Member those plays she wrote? She said she'd "ONLY WRITE PLAYS UNDER A MAN'S NAME"! But, you know, that's not why I'm calling you; Duchess!—Don't laugh, okay? I played Alice, didn't I? In *Alice in Wonderland*, didn't I play Alice?
(slight pause)
Are you laughing? Sally Moreau was the Queen of Hearts and I was Alice, right Dulcie? Stop laughing. Dulcie. Listen. OH GOD!
(she's breathing fast)
I think I'm having a heart attack!
(faster)
Hang up and call the hospital, Dulcie. Stop laughing. This isn't my big finish! I'm actually having a heart attack. Stop laughing! Stop laughing!
(she starts to hang up, grabs the arms of the chair, drops phone, grabs her chest, collapses in the chair, is very still suddenly.)
(pause)

HOUSE MANAGER
I have your coat.
(pause)

WOMAN
Someone left a folding chair in the wings.

HOUSE MANAGER
(climbing on stage)
I'm terribly sorry!

WOMAN

Don't drag my coat.

HOUSE MANAGER

(giving it to her)
That new assistant started today.
(moving into wings)
I'm really sorry!

WOMAN

Oh, could you get my pocketbook?

HOUSE MANAGER

(off)
Oh, someone left a note for you at the box office.

WOMAN

(fixing her hair, grinning)
Was it Don?

HOUSE MANAGER

(entering with pocketbook)
It was a woman. Are you going through the theater? I'll get the step unit.
(heads back into the wings)

WOMAN

Just help me to the edge.

HOUSE MANAGER

(holds out pocketbook)
Here's your pocketbook.

WOMAN

(taking it)
Do you have the note? You said someone left a note.

HOUSE MANAGER
(searches his jacket)
Yah, uh...
(pulls out a small colored envelope)

WOMAN
Read it to me.

HOUSE MANAGER
(putting on glasses)
Sure. Uh.
(looking at envelope as he takes out note)
There's nothing on the envelope; the note says:
"Sorry I can't make your rehearsal tonight.
I have a hot date at the Players Club.
Don't break your leg.
Goonie."

WOMAN
WHO?

HOUSE MANAGER
(still looking at note)
Uh, it's signed "Goonie".

WOMAN
(laughing)
Someone's playing a joke. Goonie.
(pause)

HOUSE MANAGER
I mean if somebody'd TOLD me, I would've CHECKED backstage.

WOMAN
It's my fault. I didn't tell anyone I was coming in tonight. EXCEPT Don. Help me down now.

HOUSE MANAGER
(stuffing envelope in pocket.)
Sure.
(he helps her to the edge of the stage, she sits, he jumps down)
WOMAN
See what geniuses we are.
HOUSE MANAGER
(Lifting her to the floor)
Alley-oop.
(she lands)

WOMAN
(stops)
Oh, wait. lemme change these shoes.
(she will sit on the stage.

HOUSE MANAGER
Actually, I'll uh, deal with these lights while you're doing that.
(moving)
Stay here, okay?

WOMAN
(smiling, taking off shoes)
Are you sure the cab will wait?

HOUSE MANAGER
(moving up aisle)
RAVI? Complete mercenary.

WOMAN
(perhaps in the middle of laughing)
How was I?

HOUSE MANAGER
(he stops)(pause)
I watch you every night.

WOMAN

Tonight?

HOUSE MANAGER

Just the last part. I was defrosting the refrigerator.

WOMAN

How was I?
(pause)

HOUSE MANAGER

I don't like the play.

WOMAN

Really?
(slight pause)

HOUSE MANAGER

I think it's extremely admirable for you to rehearse on your night off but I think this play is vicious. Why would you play a part like this? Do you mind my asking?

WOMAN

No.

HOUSE MANAGER

And the biography in the program's a fake: it's not even a man who wrote this play, it's a woman.

WOMAN

Really?

HOUSE MANAGER

But nobody knows who she is!

WOMAN

So you've watched me do the whole thing you said?
(slight pause)

HOUSE MANAGER

Oh, yeah. You're great!

WOMAN

(smiling)
Thanks.
(pause)

HOUSE MANAGER

(moving)
Lemme just get these lights.

WOMAN

(he goes out)(pause)
Oh, did they reserve the ticket for Don for tomorrow night?

HOUSE MANAGER

(bounding up to the light booth)
His secretary called, he wants two tickets now.

WOMAN

Really? He must be bringing a client.
(he's in the light booth)(pause)

HOUSE MANAGER

Yeah: COMPUTERIZED LIGHT BOARD—gimme a break!

WOMAN

Could you tell that I'm blind?
(pause)

HOUSE MANAGER

(tinkering)
Only a coupla times when you put your cup down on the tabl...

WOMAN
(interrupting, blushing)
RIGHT RIGHT,—I WAS SPOTTING THE TABLE WITH MY FINGER—

HOUSE MANAGER
(interrupting)
You only did it a coupla times!
(to himself)
yeah, they leave instructions but they don't tell you which BANK it's on!
(reading)
"the sound system is patched to the lights." PATCHED? So, Don hasn't seen the play yet?

WOMAN
He was very upset when he couldn't come opening night. My sister needed help with her contract.
(slight pause)

HOUSE MANAGER
He's a lawyer—Don?

WOMAN
Agent.

HOUSE MANAGER
YOUR agent?

WOMAN
I wanna make it on my own.

HOUSE MANAGER
And your sister's an actress?

WOMAN
I'll have you know my sister is a famous fashion model.
(slight pause)

HOUSE MANAGER

Really?

WOMAN

I keep telling her to come. She was crazy about *Alice in Wonderland* when we were kids.

HOUSE MANAGER

Really.

WOMAN

Oh, yeah: she used to write her own sequels—she always had to be Alice though.

HOUSE MANAGER
(almost interrupting)
I'm just gonna start throwing switches. Don't be alarmed if I get electrocuted—

WOMAN

Be careful!

HOUSE MANAGER

So, I'd recognize her if I saw her—your sister?

WOMAN

Oh sure!
(pause)
The fashion world calls her "The queen of the parting shot". It's that last look some women give you before they leave. She's famous for it! I'm told.

HOUSE MANAGER
(after a pause)
(out on the balcony, he has stopped tinkering)
Black hair?

WOMAN

Yes!

HOUSE MANAGER

Thin? Kind of a PUG nose—

WOMAN

(grinning)
See, you have seen her!
(pause)

HOUSE MANAGER

Yes. I have.
(pause)

WOMAN

Did that note say "players club"? Do you have that note?

HOUSE MANAGER

(taking it out of his pocket)
Yes.

WOMAN

Could you read it again? Do you mind?

HOUSE MANAGER

Not at all.
(reading)
"Sorry I can't make your rehearsal tonight.
I have a hot date at the Players Club.
Don't break your leg.
Goonie."
(pause)

WOMAN

Must be one of Don's friends. He's a member of the Players Club. I'm ready to go now.

HOUSE MANAGER
(moving back into the booth)
Uh, stay right there—I'm gonna hit this switch.
(he does)
It's onna DELAY—music comes on, then the lights go out. I hope.

WOMAN
(lifts herself onto the floor)
I think I can find the aisle by myself.

HOUSE MANAGER
(he runs down the stairs)
You'll hurt yourself!

WOMAN
(she's heading for a wall)
I'm not a cripple.

HOUSE MANAGER
(he has entered, he runs down the aisle)
You're about to walk into a wall!

WOMAN
(smiling)(she stops)
I knew that.
(pause)(he is with her)

HOUSE MANAGER
(holding her)
You coulda hurt yourself.

WOMAN
(pause)(stopping a moment)
Did you say you saw the woman who delivered that note?
(pause)

THE QUEEN OF THE PARTING SHOT 45

HOUSE MANAGER
I did see her, yes.
(pause)

WOMAN
Was it my sister?
(slight pause)

HOUSE MANAGER
Yes, it was.
(slight pause)

WOMAN
It's crucial to me that I'm excellent tomorrow night. Do you think I'm excellent?
(pause)

HOUSE MANAGER
(embraces her)
I think you're the sweetest woman I've ever met.
(pause)

WOMAN
But am I excellent?

HOUSE MANAGER
(he releases her and looks at her)
Very.
(pause)
C'mon.
(he will start to lead her up the aisle)

WOMAN
Will you be here tomorrow night?
(pause)

HOUSE MANAGER
(smiles)
Oh, yeah.
(music starts) (lights begin very slow fade to black)

(he leads her out)

(The play is over.)

intermission

THE AUDITION

(Intermission music is playing. A woman's voice is heard over the loudspeakers.)

WOMAN'S VOICE
(over the loudspeakers)
Would Lisa D'Angelo report backstage, please? Lisa D'Angelo?
(music continues playing)
(A minute goes by)
Would Lisa D'Angelo report backstage? Lisa D'Angelo.
(music continues)
(another minute goes by)
Uh. Is there a Jack Singleton in the audience? Would Jack Singleton report backstage, please? Jack Singleton?
(A man wearing a coat has stood in the audience, he's looking around. Suddenly he jumps on stage, goes backstage.)
(music continues)
(two minutes goes by)
(music stops, the two-minute warning has already been flashed)
Ladies and Gentlemen, as part of our intermission and second-half entertainment, we present the runner-up in the Karl D. Gruber Acting Competition. Lisa Lynne D'Angelo was the winner, but she's not here tonight. The Karl D. Gruber Acting Grant is given to that actor who best exemplifies excellence, spontaneity, technique and characterization. Karl D. Gruber said: "In all of nature, there is only one true chameleon; the perfect actor." Tonight, we present the runner-up in the Karl D. Gruber Acting Scholarship; Mister Jack Singleton.
(that man from the audience walks on stage. He's not wearing his coat. he's holding a glass of water.)
While we give Mister Singleton a moment to check his props, I will review the ground rules.

(he puts the glass down behind a curtain, goes backstage again, we will hear noise back there.)

WOMAN'S VOICE (continued)

There will be three rounds. In round one, the candidate must sing a song, and perform two acting monologues: one modern, one classical. The round is to last no longer than ten minutes. A buzzer will signal the end of each round. In round two, the candidate must introduce himself, talk a little about himself and then re-live a very personal experience. The round is fifteen minutes. In round three, the candidate must improv a situation invented on the spot by a panel of judges. Tonight, I will give Mister Singleton the situation. The last round is six minutes. May we have the house lights down, please?

(over loudspeakers continuing)(the house lights go out, the stage lights are already on)

Ready, Mr. Singleton?

JACK SINGLETON
(from backstage)
READY!

WOMAN'S VOICE
(over the loudspeaker)
Ladies and Gentlemen, the runner-up in the Karl D. Gruber Acting Scholarship, JACK SINGLETON. May we hear the buzzer please?
(the BUZZER SOUNDS)
(Jack charges onstage wearing a cowboy hat)

JACK SINGLETON
(Singing.)
"NO TWO COWBOYS ARE THE SAME
MARSHALL VISHNEE IS MY NAME!
WHEN OUTLAWS COME,
AND UNLIKE SOME,

JACK SINGLETON (continued)
I BRANDISH FIREARMS AND AIM!
OH, NO TWO COWBOYS ARE THE SAME!
MY POOR HORSE MICHAELMAS IS LAME!
MY HANDS FEEL NUMB,
I'LL CHEW MY GUM,
THIS GALLOPING THROUGH TIME IS NOT A GAME!
(he crouches, the song becomes ballad-like)
THE AESCHYLUS GALAXY I CALL HOME,
COMFY IN MY GEODISC DOME.
BUT I LOST MY NELL
DOWN A LINEAR WELL.
I DOVE IN AFTER HER AN' HELL,
HERE I AM!
THE NINETEENTH CENTURY!
THE NINETEENTH CENTURY!
(stands)
IT'S SMELLY, IT'S DIRTY,
IT'S ONLY FIVE-THIRTY!
THERE'S ABSOLUTELY NOTHING TO DO!
IF I COULD FIND HER,
I'D BIND HER
AN' CARRY HER HOME;
BUT HOW?
I NEED A TEMPORAL STORM,
WHEN THE AIR GETS WARM,
A TRI-LOCATIONAL VACUUM, AND A
COWBOY NAMED NORM!
HE'LL TAKE MY PLACE,
IN VERTICAL SPACE;
I CAN'T GET BACK WITHOUT HIS FORM,
AND SO—
AND SO—
NO TWO COWBOYS ARE THE SAME!

JACK SINGLETON (continued)
NORM WILL HAVE TO TAKE MY NAME!
SO, WHEN OUTLAWS COME,
AND UNLIKE SOME,
HE'LL BRANDISH FIREARMS AND AIM!
HE'LL BRANDISH FIREARMS AND AIM!

(pause)
(he tosses the cowboy hat into the wings)

My first monologue is from *Richard IV*.

(he takes out a red-stained handkerchief, ties it around his head)

"Brave Otto's warning: tis a remembrance: twas full
Three score an' eight and I was but a yeoman:
The war was not yet ripe.
In full faculty could I discourse,
And in a mead hall grinning would I sing of it,
But here, on Lambsworth Field, with stench of death,
Shall I muster but a shadow of the tale.
What I hear, cousins, is the woman betrayed him:
The serving girl! O righteous villainy that
Masquerades in pleasing form! Anna, the serving
Girl; of Flemish stock; those great barbarians
Who crossed the sea, their ambitions dashed
By Huns, forced to servitude, herded as bison,
Smitten in the prime of ambition, she, Anna,
Granddaughter of misery, of lost hope, she who
Betrayed brave Otto.
I interrupt my tale, cousins; my wound o'ertakes me,
My mind aloof, my heart resolute, my soul holding fast,
As I tell you the warning. I must sit.

(he does)(pause)

The second Abyssinian war was nearing end,
The land was ripe, the children healthy,
Brave Otto's forces laying siege in Pellopenesia;
That last bastion. We had won, cousins!

THE AUDITION

JACK SINGLETON (continued)
Twas during this siege that Otto took ill with
Poisoning
Some say twas the food, but she, cousins, she nursed him
Back to life; well, then, he went mad for her!
He'd stage showy parades an' lead her at the front,
Bedecked all in local finery!
He'd hold huge galas in her honor, then our chief
Commander went to him saying 'Brave Otto, you have
Far too much reverie for someone who's supposed to be
Conducting a siege of Pellopenesia!'
Well, cousins, as you know, Otto snapped.
He murdered all his generals, and still held that
Gala for which he is now famous.
But he warns us in his farewell address,
Just before the guards rushed him an' cut out his
Intestines:
'The serving girl, he said, 'beware the serving girl!
She is the vilest creature to walk the planet!
She will sponge your weaknesses til she is your
Weakness!'
And that, cousins, is precisely when they rushed him
And cut out his intestines.
(pause)
I am dying. I leave you Lambsworth field, and
Brave Otto's warning
Before you battle the Hun.
Take both from my heart.
I die, a soldier."
(he dies)
(pause)
(he gets up, dusting himself off, he takes off bandage, he takes out a pair of glasses)

My second monologue is from *Modern Problems*.

JACK SINGLETON (continued)
(he turns away for a moment, then turns back, wearing glasses)
"I heard that, Joan.
(looking off)
Hey, Billy, pipe down willya?
(back to Joan)
I'd rather say this privately to you—
(looking elsewhere)
thanks, Mike, this is between me and Joan.
(back to her)
Look, Joan, when the kids're sick, or some SCHOOL THING happens, I'm right there for the team. How dare you tell other people I'm having an affair! You women DO NOT realize how much we men like having sex! You try to attach all these DIVISIVE, long-term plans to it. Sure, we'll make you our MOTHERS, but that has nothing to do with sex! You get MULTIPLE orgasms. Boy, if I could shoot my wad twenty times a night I'd make Christ look like an epileptic! What? What does the Senate race have to do with this? Look, I'm LYING. I WOULD NEVER CHEAT ON MARY. I KISS EVERY ONE OF HER GOD DAMN TOES EVERY SINGLE GOD DAMN MORNING! SURE SHE'S GOT FLAB, IT'S ARTISTIC, IT'S BOTTICELLI, ALL THOSE GREAT PAINTERS WHO LOVED FAT WOMEN. GET THAT DISGUSTING LOOK OFF YOUR FACE!
(looking off)
C'MON, BILLY. GIVE JENNY THE DAMN TOY!
(back to her)
Sometimes I'd like to murder those kids with a pick axe. Will you look at yourself, Joan? How old're you? —fifty? Sorry, thirty-four. Well, hmmm. No, well, you DO have a nice body: good yubbies. Tell me, you like being mounted from the back, right? What?
(looking off)
GET OFF OF JENNY, BILLY, WHAT'RE YOU, CRAZY?

THE AUDITION

JACK SINGLETON (continued)
(back to her)

I have a lot to lose, Joan. I mean I'm TRYING TO PICTURE MYSELF IN THE MOTEL ROOM WITH YOU: I SEE A FULL-LENGTH MIRROR, BEETHOVEN'S BLASTING, I PICTURE IT, JOAN, BUT I JUST DON'T FEEL IT! WHAT THE HELL CAN I SAY! But, I will hire you for the Senate race. I know that's why you cornered me.

Am I right?
(holding out his hand)
WELCOME ABOARD!"
(pause)
Thank you.
(Takes off glasses. Takes a stopwatch out of his pocket as he heads into the wings. A BUZZER SOUNDS. He emerges with a folding chair, he's looking at his stopwatch.)

Just made it.
(puts stopwatch away)

Uh, I'm gonna try'n follow this format as closely as I can; this is obviously different. I know there's a play on after this: I mean I usually getta bare stage. Okay, uh, hi, I'm Jack Singleton.
(placing chair down)

Welcome to round two. This is strange; having to repeat my spontaneousness for you. ANYWAY, HI!
(sits)

BOY, HOW 'BOUT THAT LAST PLAY, HUH? WEIRD CITY, NO? I may be from Pratt, West Virginia, but I didn't understand DICK. So okay, so she's BLIND, I got that, but WHAT'S WITH THE SISTER? THE SISTER'S SEEING THE BOYFRIEND? THE SISTER WROTE THE PLAY? WHY DON'T THEY TELL US? AND WHAT'S THE POINT EVEN IF THE SISTER DID WRITE THE PLAY? SHE'S THE QUEEN OF THE PARTING SHOT—SO WHAT? The guy who played the house manager was great, though, I thought.

JACK SINGLETON (continued)
(slight pause)

Anyway, hi. I didn't even know I was gonna get to go on tonight. I brought my good-luck stopwatch, maybe that's what did it. Good thing I left my cowboy hat here last night. They let me rehearse here last night; in case I had to go on. Good thing I left my cowboy hat. OKAY—Jack Singleton, Pratt, West Virginia. I'm thirty-two, never married, yet eminently eligible, ladies, pay attention. Hey, I was watching this HBO special in my hotel room on Women's Sexuality; they showed a bunch of middle-aged women in this CLASS, RELAXING WITH EACH OTHER. I'm using the word RELAXING because I'm a gentleman, but MY GOD! WHERE HAVE I BEEN FOR TEN YEARS? THAT'S OUTRAGEOUS! So, okay, so Mrs. Etta Marble needs to UNWIND, she's got PROBLEMS, but WHAT ABOUT THE LOOK ON MISTER MARBLE'S FACE WHEN HE WARMS UP THE OLE TV? I wouldn't wanna be him.

(slight pause)

Me, I'm single. As I said, I'm from Pratt. I was born in Bertko, West Virginia. We moved to Pratt when I was seven. I'm named after my uncle Jack Singleton; a coal miner turned insurance salesman, which, if you know Uncle Jack, is the same thing. he's well over six feet, great bushy beard, always wears a Hell's Angels jacket, he has four of them, never married, an' he has this great hacking cough—you always know when he's around. And the only relative to stand behind my decision to become an actor. I'm proud to be named after him.

(pause)

I'm more nervous than I thought I'd be.

(he leans into the wings)

I hid a glass of water back here. Here it is.

(he sits back down with the glass of water)

I think it's the room. It's a dry room. Because I never getta dry mouth, but when I was rehearsing here last night I noticed that.

(sips)

JACK SINGLETON (continued)

That's why I had this glass ready. I mean, I thought of it when they called my name tonight. I thought "hey, I better have a glass of water ready."
(puts glass back in the wings)
But, y'know, my life wasn't always this exciting.
(slight pause)
Apparently it's becoming fashionable to trash your childhood, rat out on your parents. Well, MY dad only beat me when he was sober, so the moment I'd get my allowance I'd run into town, find the local bum, an' BRIBE him into buying me blended whiskey so I could keep ole dad smiling. Then he'd start singing at the top of his lungs, his veins'd pop out, dogs'd start barking, dad'd just sing louder. He hadda general store for a coupla years, but he couldn't stay focused on it. Some people're just born pissed off. That was dad. BOB SINGLETON'S GENERAL STORE. The town fathers tried running him out because he wouldn't kiss their butts. He'd take me to town meetings with him DRUNK OUT OF HIS MIND. We'd sit way in the back, he'd let all the town fathers speak their peace, then he'd slowly raise his hand. Now, when I say he was drunk, I mean GONE, OUT, you know what I'm talking about: your mind's in another place, your brain is BURIED UNDER ALL THIS STUFF, my dad had this knack for looking stone-faced, LIKE HE WAS SERIOUSLY CONSIDERING A PROBLEM: so he's raising his hand, an' some councilman says, "AH, LET'S HEAR FROM BOB SINGLETON, OWNER OF BOB SINGLETON'S GENERAL STORE." My father's standing by this time.
(is standing)
He'd let a long pause go by, then he'd say, "I JUST WANNA KNOW ONE THING! JUST ONE THING!" One of them says "And what might that be, Mister Singleton?"
(imitates his father again)
" I WANNA KNOW WHAT THE HELL IS GOING ON HERE! WOULD SOMEBODY IN THIS ROOM TELL ME WHAT THE HELL IS GOING ON HERE!" He'd stay standing, expecting

JACK SINGLETON (continued)

an answer. One of them finally says "Mister Singleton raises a KEY issue" my father interrupts "THAT'S NOT WHAT I'M ASKING YOU! I JUST WANNA KNOW WHAT THE HELL IS GOING ON HERE!"

(pause)

    That was my dad.

(pause.

    He died in a skiing accident.

(short pause)

    Not really an accident, though.

(pause)

    I got this long letter from one of his buddies: Bert Magnusson, or something. I was in business school at the time, I skipped the funeral, an' ole Bert sent me this nasty letter, well it started out nasty but it ends with a vivid description of the accident.

(short pause)

    Apparently, they were on a Knights of Columbus retreat, or something. Bert's brother-in-law ran this LODGE up in Vermont. It was all an excuse for a BOOZE FEST, is what it was. Now this lodge is near the top of Mount Ricky, or something, which has a very nice slope most good skiers can handle, BUT ON THE OTHER SIDE IS DEAD MAN'S CLIFF; a one hundred foot arcing slope which descends to a LEDGE two thousand feet above tree tops.

(short pause)

    So the boys get up to the lodge right before a storm hits. They're getting snowed in, but ole Bert's brother-in-law's got tons of supplies: whiskey, dirty movies, toilet paper, potato chips. Bert said about two a.m. Dad challenged everybody to a singing contest, an' sometime right after that, an enormous argument broke out. Aggie Kondak accused Johnny Muskoolo of sleeping with his wife. Dad was best friends with Johnny. The one fact you can take home with you tonight about my father was that no matter how drunk he was, LOYALTY was number one. Period.

JACK SINGLETON (continued)

(short pause)

So the storm is raging outside, and inside the yelling and screaming is getting violent. Bert said Aggie started calling dad a loser, telling him he'd pissed his life away, starts citing EXAMPLES, an' some of the other guys start laughin' at dad, then JOHNNY turns on dad, tellin' him Aggie's right: he DID piss his life away. So dad grabs his coat an' runs outside. Bert runs out after him, but the snow is blinding, the winds're knocking him over, he's yellin' my dad's name but all he gets is a mouthful of blizzard. So Bert runs back inside an' punches Johnny in the face. Most of the other guys were passing out. Bert said he grabbed a bottle of Wild Turkey an' sat down near a window, waiting for dad to come back.
(pause)

An hour goes by. The storm is over. Bert said he tried to organize a search party but everybody'd passed out. So, he grabs a lantern, an' goes outside.
(short pause)

Bert said he could see faded tracks in the snow; leading to a barn out back. Lights'd been turned on in the barn, he said the doors were wide open, he figured dad musta passed out in there. he started callin' his name again. He said a lotta equipment had been thrown around, skis ripped down from their racks. Bert said he saw a spot in the middle of the barn where dad musta sat down, or something. I don't know how Bert figured that out, but he did see ski tracks at the far end, leading out a side door which had also been thrown open. Dad musta put on a pair of skis.
(short pause)

Now, to get UP to Dead Man's Cliff, Bert says you gotta climb this steep hill, with tree branches whacking you in the face. The trees're bunched together, so if you were climbing it wearing skis, it'd be like this maze where you have to go, say, ten feet to your right, then ten feet to your left. Even though it was twenty below, Bert said he'd already broken a sweat. He kept callin' dad's name, hoping he might be just up ahead.
(short pause)

JACK SINGLETON (continued)

Bert says when you finally get to the top, you think you're in a field. It's all darkness in front of you. Bert said he was holding up his lantern, he said he took a coupla steps forward, but stopped. He could feel the ground beginning to descend. An abyss was opening up in front of him. He saw the ski tracks still in front of him. He heard only great wind. He stood there a long time. Whatever had happened was over.
(pause)

I remember the first time I read Bert's letter, I put it down at this point.
(pause)

I had been carrying the letter around with me all day. Bert had crammed three pieces of legal-size paper into an average-sized envelope. I was dreading the thought of having to read it. I tossed it away down a laundry chute: I was living in a dormitory at the time, then about three a.m. I hear someone knocking on my door, very quietly. I hear a woman's voice, I recognize the voice; this chippy Asian girl from the second floor, been trying to get into my pants for months. What does she do, hang out in the laundry room all day? I let her slide it under the door. I didn't respond.
(pause)

So when I put down Bert's letter, I remembered the Asian girl. And I called her up. "YOU FUCKIN' CUNT!" Pardon my Japanese, but I was really pissed! "YOU FUCKIN' CUNT! I'M GONNA FLUNK MY LAST CHANCE EXAM BECAUSE OF YOU! I'M STUDYING MY BRAINS OUT AND YOU SLIDE THIS PIECE OF SHIT LETTER UNDER MY DOOR! I THREW IT AWAY, DIDN'T I? I'm GONNA BE UP ALL NIGHT NOW!" An' she didn't hang up. I did.
(pause)

In the morning, a search party combed the base of Dead Man's Cliff. Bert said everyone was terrified. They were looking for arms or legs. They had long lost the big picture.

THE AUDITION

JACK SINGLETON (continued)
(short pause)

They found nothing at the base of the cliff. Nor in the woods. No trace of dad anywhere. Finally, someone suggested they re-trace dad's steps. Thanks to Bert, they did. And now, in the daylight, Bert looked into the abyss and saw a way out. He spotted a left-hand turn down the cliff, a veer-off. See, if you look down it, it's like a ski slope, except there's a left-hand turn between the rock and the cliff. But Bert said once it took the turn, you couldn't see where it went.
(short pause)

So Bert goes back down to the barn an' gets into a pair of skis. He finds a huge coil of rope an' proceeds to climb back up.
(short pause)

Okay, so he ties himself up, an' gets Johnny and Aggie an' all the other guys to lower him down the slope, he's gonna follow dad's tracks to this veer-off, it's the only answer .
(short pause)

Well, there's a tree down this veer-off. it's the only tree on the plateau; it's the only tree on Dead Man's Cliff. And dad hit it.
(short pause)

Bert said the entire front of dad's body had embedded in the tree; he musta hit it goin' about seventy, maybe more. Bert said he tried to call out to the others, but he was chokin' on his tears. he said if there was a positive side to the whole thing it was that dad couldn't have seen the tree comin'. I mean, by the time he took that veer-off, he musta thought he was already in the air; he thought he'd reach the sky, he thought he'd made it.
(pause)

After they buried him, Uncle Jack came up on a train. I still hadn't gotten Bert's letter yet. I was studying for that exam.
(pause)

He was mad at me, Uncle Jack. He said my mother had been through enough. Why wasn't I home with my mother, taking care of her. I started yellin' "WHAT THE HELL DOES MY MOTHER HAVE TO DO WITH THIS?" He grabbed me by the throat.

JACK SINGLETON (continued)
(THE BUZZER SOUNDS. He takes out his stopwatch, looks at it, puts it away.)
Not bad.

WOMAN'S VOICE
(over the loudspeakers)
May we have the house lights up please?
(house lights go up)
Ladies and Gentlemen, before we begin this third round, you should know that several top movie agents are here tonight, and this last round, the improv round, is what they really came to see. The Karl D. Gruber Acting Grant provides an exciting launching pad for its winners. Mister Singleton will, no doubt, be meeting with these agents as soon as he is finished. Are you ready, Mr. Singleton?

JACK SINGLETON
(smiling)
I hope so.

WOMAN'S VOICE
(over the loudspeakers)
Here's your situation: let's go back in time twenty-five minutes ago; let's say you're just getting ready to come on.
(Jack moves into the wings to retrieve his cowboy hat)
You're wearing your cowboy hat, you're standing in the wings. I'm just about to introduce you.

JACK SINGLETON
(having re-entered)
Should you be letting everyone in on this?

WOMAN'S VOICE
(over the loudspeaker)
Unbeknownst to anyone,

THE AUDITION

WOMAN'S VOICE (continued)
(Jack has picked up his folding chair)
you've murdered Lisa Lynne D'Angelo.
(Jack drops the folding chair on the stage)
(pause)
(Jack quickly picks it up, runs backstage, we can't see him)

For the benefit of our audience, Lisa Lynne D'Angelo is the top recipient of the Karl D. Gruber Scholarship. She was supposed to perform tonight. She didn't show up. We can't find her. Mister Singleton, let's say that you've murdered her. I'll introduce you again, Mister Singleton. The buzzer will be your cue. Only this time, your guilt is bothering you so much, that you break character, you behave irrationally, you sabotage yourself. You have six minutes. May we have the house lights down please?
(they go down)
Ready, Mister Singleton?
(pause)
Are you ready Mister Singleton?

JACK SINGLETON
(offstage)(quietly)
Yes.

WOMAN'S VOICE
(over the loudspeakers)
Ladies and gentlemen, the runner-up in the Karl D. Gruber Acting Scholarship: Jack Singleton! May we hear the buzzer please?
(THE BUZZER SOUNDS. Jack comes bursting out of the wings. he's wearing the cowboy hat, and his coat)

JACK SINGLETON
(entering, dancing)(singing)
"NO TWO COWBOYS ARE THE SAME!
MARSHALL KRUSCHIEV IS MY NAME!
OH, SNOW SHOE COWBOYS'RE DISSIMILAR!
MY POOR WHORE D'ANGELO IS MAIMED
(he stops and tosses his hat into the wings)

JACK SINGLETON (continued)

My first monologue is from Singleton the Third.
(taking out bandage and falling to the floor)

"Brave Otto's warning, the girl. What was I talking about? BRAVE OTTO. I think he was a fag, what's with all those parties? I like ruffled shirts as much as any man but ENOUGH IS ENOUGH! Beware the serving girl! And that's when they rushed him with those chainsaws. I die...a soldier.

(dies)
(way in the distance, a police car siren is heard)
(Jack doesn't move, he's still lying there)
(the police siren is fading, it's going away)
(slight pause)
(Jack jumps up quickly, ripping off the bandage)

My second monologue is from *Modern Problems*.
(he turns his back on audience)(now turning)

I heard that, Joan.
(yelling off)

KICK HER IN THE FACE, BILLY! DIDN'T I TEACH YOU ANYTHING?
(looking back)

Mike, get the fuck outta here, okay?
(to Joan)

Y'know what your problem is, Joan? You gotta BIG MOUTH, A BIG FUCKIN' MOUTH!
(looking off)

THAT'S RIGHT, BILLY, NOW RIP ALL HER CLOTHES OFF WITH YOUR FINGERNAILS!
(to Joan)

You talk too much, Joan. You're a yapper. A yappy YAPPER. YAP YAP YAP YAP YAP YAP YAP YAP YAP YAP—"
(suddenly breaks character)

C'MON, THIS ISN'T GONNA WORK!
(short pause)

JACK SINGLETON (continued)
(to us)

In the actual Karl D. Gruber Auditions, they hand you the situation onna piece of paper. They don't YELL IT OUT in front of everybody. It radically alters the situation if you ALREADY KNOW THAT I KILLED HER.
(another police siren is heard in the distance. JACK runs into the wings)
(pause)
(the sirens fade, it's going away)
(Jack emerges from the wings, with the folding chair, he smiles)

Anyway, HI. Uh, I usually getta bare stage. Boy, how about that last play, huh? I saw this HBO special on WOMEN WHO MASTURBATE TOGETHER. Me, I'm single. I was named after my Uncle Jack Singleton. What a guy. Uncle Jack. Oh, I didn't tell you, HE gave me my stopwatch. Uncle Jack. When I told him about the Karl Gruber auditions; y'know with these FUCKED UP RULES—he said he was gonna BE HERE TONIGHT. I mean he sent me the stopwatch, didn't her? I figured he wasn't mad anymore. Remember I told you he grabbed me? Remember when he came up on the train? WHAT THE FUCK DOES MY MOTHER HAVE TO DO WITH THIS?
(adding quickly)

OKAY, I did it. I'll play. I murdered Lisa D'Angelo.
(short pause)

Sound irrational? It's not.
(short pause)

I'm sure not gonna tell you HOW I did it! —You want REASONS? —Remember the Asian girl?—That's PROVIDENCE, man!—I THREW THE FUCKIN' LETTER AWAY! THAT'S LIKE THE TREE! LISA D'ANGELO, GET IT? SHE SUCKED! I SAW HER AUDITION—IT'S LIKE THE ASIAN GIRL—"SO OPEN, SO NATURAL". I SAW THE JUDGES' FACES: THEY

JACK SINGLETON (continued)
LOVED HER! SHE HAD NO TECHNIQUE, NO VERSATILITY! Y'KNOW WHY MY DAD KILLED HIMSELF?— JOHNNY! WHEN JOHNNY TURNED ON HIM—JUST LIKE THE JUDGES—I'M THE FUCKIN' WINNER! THAT'S WHY THEY'RE TRYIN' TO SCREW ME TONIGHT! SHE'S NOT SUPPOSED TO YELL OUT THE SITUATION! TALK ABOUT RE-LIVING A PERSONAL EXPERIENCE!—REMEMBER WHEN SHE SLID THE LETTER UNDER MY DOOR?—I COULDA STILL TOSSED IT OUT!—BUT I GOT AN IMPULSE!—NO PLAN YET—I READ IT, I PUT IT DOWN, I CHEW OUT THE CHINK. I'M TAKING THE LEFT TURN, I'M GONNA BE AN ACTOR; IT'S JUST LIKE DAD PUTTIN' ON THE SKIS!

(moves)

HE'S SITTIN' ON THE FLOOR, HE'S GOIN' THROUGH WITH IT, HE CLIMBS TO THE TOP, HE'S SINGIN' "WHAT THE HELL IS GOIN'"—HE STOPS AN' FACES THE ABYSS!— SURE—THIS IS A GREAT PLAN! HE PUSHES OFF HARD!

(pause)

That was definitely six minutes.

(slight pause) (a police siren is heard close by)
(he's fishing in his pockets for the stopwatch)

WHAT'RE YOU, TRYIN' TO SABOTAGE ME! YOU TRYIN' TO HUMILIATE ME?

(he's searching the wings)

WHERE'S MY FUCKIN' STOPWATCH?

(he's offstage and making a lot of noise)(he runs onstage, looking)

DID I DROP IT? YOU FUCKED ME UP, LADY, YOU REALLY DID! SHIT!

(he dives off the stage, runs to side door and opens it)
(BUZZER SOUNDS.) (he slams the door behind him, he's gone)

WOMAN'S VOICE
(over the loudspeakers)
Fade the lights please.
(the lights begin fading to black)
Ladies and Gentlemen, that was Jack Singleton. The runner-up in the Karl D. Gruber Acting Scholarship. We now continue with our second-half entertainment.
Thank you.
(the room is black)
(the sirens scream past the building)
(pause)
(the sirens are fading away)

(The play is over.)

THE AWARD

(Police sirens fading in the distance. Lights come up slowly. A man is sitting in an armchair, wearing a smoking jacket. Near him is a table with a phone.)

MAN

This scene in particular is what I was referring to—there's a door over there and in a minute his mother's walking in because there was this bit at the dinner table. They've had a dinner party: sort of *Dinner at 8*. But it's more Gurney than Coward and this chap talks to the audience all the time, you see, that's the CONVENTION and there was this terrible argument at the dinner table and most of the guests have left and his mother is seeing them off apologizing and clucking and he's here in the sitting room talking to the audience because it's his point of view we've got. He's aging, that's how his sister-in-law describes it; and this business friend made a faggot remark at the table. That's what started it. Kind of a reuniony-type dinner. he's been away on sabbatical, he's got money but he teaches at a Jesuit college, only on sabbatical this year and this reunion dinner was his mother's idea to get them all together again. That's why it's like Gurney, but the MOMENT WE'RE BUILDING to is HERE in the sitting room where he's talking to the audience while his mother is saying goodbye at the front door. He can hear them all leaving. He had been abroad because there was almost a SCANDAL with a sophomore named Charles—a cherubic brainy-type which was revelatory, I mean he wasn't mincing his way through life and suddenly he's forty. This chap is BLIND to himself, that's more like Coward: blind to himself; and this Charles incident launched the sabbatical. I mean it was HIS idea to go abroad and once in Milano he entertained suicide but he was using the wrong reasons. the Charles incident was revelatory but the outburst, the explosion, could not come on that campus night in the library nor in Milano at a hotel window because no one else knew, and this dinner party seemed a good idea, a return to normalcy. Now

MAN (continued)
you've got to imagine this chap in the right way. there can be a million reasons for putting off personal relationships and if you're smart and ambitious and quasi-wealthy you've got a head start. Why should I apologize? This guy is talented. He's got this marvelous monologue on the phone with some Spanish airlines person and he's talking to the audience at the same time and he destroys his brother-in-law who walks in. I mean you know this guy isn't a loser. His mother puts him AT THE HEAD OF THE TABLE DURING DINNER. So he owns the SCENE. You know what I'm saying? And when he's talking to the audience he's bringing them along with him. He's not just commenting on the action, he's got us in the moment with him and when the business friend makes the faggot remark he turns to us and says "he's talking about me!" See, we're right there with him: "he's talking about me!" Now we're not sure if everyone sitting at the table has overheard him talking to us but then on the third time we are sure.
(short pause)

He's talking about me. Filled to the brim at this table was his happiness; his sisters who adored him, his brother who respected him and his mother, his closest friend, and remember the million reasons for putting off personal relationships because A CLOSE FAMILY IS A GOOD EXCUSE. They know bullshit about you by this time; they think you're still fourteen . They forget you've got your room and your own phone. THEY'RE JUST FAMILY. But to him they were his rock. He left Milano and the suicide note to COME HERE TONIGHT AND HAVE DINNER WITH MY FAMILY. Now there were SEVERAL events in his twenties and thirties. SEVERAL moments with women which were incomprehensible, genuinely puzzling. Some involving NUDITY which baffled him, the touch of women, the softness. Yes a feeling of friendship. But NEVER LUST, YET HE KNEW HE BURNED. THEN CHARLES AND FINALLY MILANO! God I've been that alone!
(short pause)

MAN (continued)

The guests are saying their final goodbyes to Mother at the front door and he's planted himself here in the sitting room, pretending to read a magazine. He's as successful as he ever wanted; his mother stressed education and responsibility. It's not as if he was waiting for something else but now in this room with the sisters putting on their coats and his brother casually making his excuses IT ALL SEEMED MEANINGLESS because no one knew him. He wanted distance, but not like this and not tonight. Please God not tonight.

"Why is she taking so long saying good night. What are they saying to each other? I DON'T KNOW why I said it. I just said he's talking about me. I blurted it out. Why should they attach meaning to it. I wasn't trying to break up the party. It's not as if they knew about the suicide note. And Charles is special, he's just special. That's my business. I wasn't trying to hurt anyone!"

Not that this audience can be sympathetic; how can they? They're accomplices. He speaks to them openly, the words from the hallway casting a spell as he speaks. There's our sister Ruth: "He's still not feeling well, take care of him, Mother." And Mother consoling. Now Alice; "he's sick." But kindly. And Mother consoling. And now left alone with brother Ted, the two lone figures in the hallway, and Teddy whispering, and mother whispering. I've stopped speaking and am reading this magazine; the whispering flooding the sitting room, the magazine a blur of color, and Teddy—
(whispering)

"He never told me" and silence.
(very slight pause)
And Mother—
(whispering)
"I've always known."
(very slight pause)
The magazine is falling from his lap.
(he's miming the magazine)

MAN (continued)

And Mother again—
(whispering)
"I've always known."
(very slight pause)
(quietly)

Father's death had been by slow cancer—painful, the long afternoons in his study where he described his pain, had learned to visualize his pain, his dreams all having one villain who tore down the grand castle, attacked the peaceful family on the beach, the pain now human to him. Sometimes distant sometimes close, and in that study when the day still had hours he would read Thomas Hardy aloud until the imagery suited his mood and the pain would come, often in droves, and he would take in his breath fast and force a smile until the invasion subsided. No words could help him, no loving gesture. he was alone with pain and on one Wednesday with *Jude the Obscure.* pouring forth the final invasion succeeded—the breath came fast and went.
(short pause)

And mother was somewhere in that room. She could have said it then. With father dead and all the old ghosts of masculinity and sports teams and fairy behavior and sissy boy dead and buried, SHE COULD HAVE SAID IT THEN. This night was far too late and much too much a betrayal, especially with Ted who knew him less than anyone. Now, with the whispering and the goodbyes, where there might be an explosion could only come resignation, emptiness! He knew for the first time how his father must've felt on that Wednesday when the breath came fast and went.
(short pause)

He could hear his mother's footsteps across the hall. She was coming this way. She's about to walk through that door.
(the phone rings, he starts)
(pause)
(he answers phone)

THE AWARD

MAN (continued)

Yes.
(short pause)
I'm fine.
(short pause)
Why were you all worried? I said I'm fine.
(short pause)
Because I didn't WANT a drink. I lost, didn't I? Why would I want to go out?
(short pause)
Well, Tyrone, I don't think it's FIXED; would you have said that if I'd won?
(short pause)
I know what you meant. Forgive me.
(short pause)
I don't want a drink. I have to go.
(short pause)
Goodbye.
(hangs up)(pause)
I wasn't gonna take this part. I LOVE doing soaps.
(slight pause)
I was looking for a breakthrough role.
(short pause)
I was Doctor Peterson, or Doctor Mathewson and always friendly and always with some female companion. Old ladies love me and say so in letters. GREAT MONEY in SOAPS AND SECURITY—but lurking somewhere was the breakthrough role. And it WASN'T just that playing a faggot would cost me, it's that scene with the mother. I mean you've got to really play that scene. And I kept thinking, they're gonna know for sure during that scene: all those matinee ladies and casting directors and middle-aged men. They're gonna know for sure it's just some aging faggot who's been type-cast but KNOWING that, I could play the scene fully, or so I thought. But then the director said "I don't believe you." Then he'd

MAN (continued)

have me sit down and "I don't believe you." And then he'd have me cry more and "I don't believe you." Then he wanted me to play the opposite of what I was thinking which threw me because here I am with this revelatory role and how it parallels my own life I can't tell you and he wanted the opposite. I SHOULD HAVE WON TONIGHT!

(pause)

Even with that hindrance I played the scene beautifully. Even on that Awards show tonight just that scene brought the house down. "I HAVE NEVER KNOW BETRAYAL LIKE THIS" and mother bursting into tears "I SHOULD HAVE DIED IN MILANO, IS THAT WHAT YOU WANT?" She, now a crumpled mess on the floor—"Oh, Mother, you've always known? Well, I've always wanted you to know! LOOK AT ME—Look at your son. I have no friends. No one knows me. I'm so alone!"

(pause)

I should have won tonight.

(short pause)

I can't go back to the soaps now.

(short pause)

Not now.

(short pause)

Some of those women used to ask me out. I'd go. I had to.

(short pause)

I'm the faggot who lost now.

(short pause)

But that scene brought the house down.

(the phone rings)
(pause)(he doesn't move)
(short pause)
(he answers phone)

Yes.

(short pause)

MAN (continued)

Hello, mother.
(pause)
No, I'm fine.
(pause)
But I didn't want you to fly in. Why should you feel bad about it? You saw it on television.
(pause)
It's my own tuxedo. What?
(pause)
No, she's on another soap opera, they just fixed us up for the night. Public relations. you know?
(pause)
Yes, she's very nice.
(pause)
Oh, I knew I didn't have a chance. You know how these things are.
(short pause)
Mrs. Bench said what?
(pause)
It's an excerpt from the play.
(short pause)
She said he's what?
(short pause)
Well you tell Mrs. Bench it's a little more universal than a sissy boy with problems. It's a wonderful play.
(pause)
No. As I said, she's on another soap opera. I don't know her that well, mother.
(pause)
She's very pretty.
(short pause)
Her name's Diana.
(short pause)

MAN (continued)

My schedule is so busy, though. Listen, I have company; I'll phone you in the morning.
(pause)

Just some friends. They're waiting for me to get off the line.
(pause)

I'm fine mother. I didn't want the damn award anyway! You know how people talk!
(pause)

That's right. So I'll phone you. Yes.
(pause)

Right. Goodbye, mother.
(hangs up)(pause)
(he sits looking out at us)

Now.
(slight pause)

Where was I?
(pause)
(lights fade to black)

(The play is over.)

PROPERTY PLOT

ONE FOR THE MONEY

MAN
Index Cards
Eight or nine one dollar bills
Letter from Ontario

MOROCCAN TRAVEL GUIDE

FEMALE STAND-UP
Cordless Microphone

THE QUEEN OF THE PARTING SHOT

WOMAN
Telephone
Cup of tea
Newspaper

HOUSE MANAGER
Note
Folding chair (offstage)

THE AUDITION

JACK SINGLETON
Stopwatch
Bandage
Folding chair

THE AWARD

MAN
Telephone

COSTUME PLOT

ONE FOR THE MONEY

MAN
Suit(conservative)
Cats Mask
Coat

MOROCCAN TRAVEL GUIDE

FEMALE STAND-UP
Tight leather purple outfit(pants)
Black boots
Wrist watch

THE QUEEN OF THE PARTING SHOT

WOMAN
Faded flower dress
Wig
Old lady shoes

HOUSE MANAGER
Shirt and tie
Vest
Woman's coat(hers)

THE AUDITION

JACK SINGLETON
Leather jacket
Shirt and tie
Dress pants

Boots
Cowboy hat
Spectacles (for Modern Problems)

THE AWARD

MAN
Smoking Jacket
Bow tie and dress shirt
Dress shoes

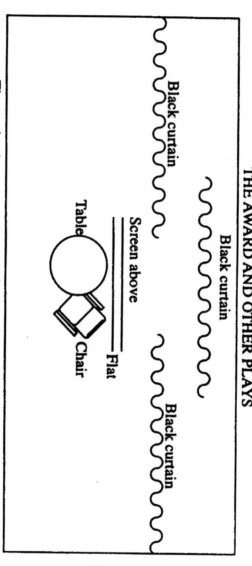

BASIC SET DESIGN
THE AWARD AND OTHER PLAYS

The projection screen appears for <u>Moroccan Travel Guide</u> only.

NOTES FROM THE ORIGINAL NEW YORK PRODUCTION

It was essential going in, that no actor DOUBLE, each play is its own universe. The audience would become confused, and the concept goes against the nature of the plays.

Generally speaking, <u>ONE FOR THE MONEY</u> should MOVE. It really shouldn't run much longer than fifteen minutes.

<u>THE QUEEN OF THE PARTING SHOT</u> is after all a memory play, stream of consciousness, and finally, a mystery.

<u>THE AUDITION</u> went through many changes, and I am grateful to James Farrell and Trip Hamilton for paving the way to our final version, as originated by David Valcin.

<u>THE AWARD</u> was originally commissioned by the Actors Collective for a benefit performance for "God's Love We Deliver." That organization's work with AIDS patients serves as a great inspiration and Marcus Powell's performance was a strong factor in my wanting to expand the experience, and write four other plays to go with it.